PICTURING SCOTLAND

DUNDEE & ANGUS

NESS PUBLISHING

2 A panoramic view of Dundee taken from Fife across the Firth of Tay, with the Tay Road Bridge on the left. The Dundee waterfront is undergoing major redevelopment and by the time this book is

DUNDEE & ANGUS

published at least one of the tower blocks in this picture will have been demolished.

Welcome to Dundee & Angus!

Dundee, Scotland's fourth city, stands proudly on the north bank of the Firth of Tay. Covering just 21 square miles, by area it is the country's smallest Unitary Authority, but is second only to Glasgow in terms of population density. The city's beginnings go back to the 11th century and it was given a charter by King William in 1191. This granted certain rights to the town, such as the right to establish local government and operate a court. Charters also allowed or paved the way for greater commerce and by the 13th century Dundee held an annual fair – which in those days was more of a market than an entertainment. The development of a harbour stimulated trade, such that by the 14th century Dundee was one of Scotland's largest towns.

The following three centuries saw a pattern of growth and setbacks, of prosperity gained then lost to circumstances such as epidemics, wars with England and, perhaps most destructively, the Civil War. Dundee suffered at the hands of both sides; in 1644 the Royalist Marquis of Montrose besieged it and in 1651 Cromwell's forces captured it. Their pillaging cost the lives of up to 2,000 of a population of 12,000. It took Dundee a century to recover. The city's growth since about 1800 is said to have been built on 'Jute, Jam and Journalism'. Jams date from 1797 when James Keiller & Son established a preserves factory. Jute began to be imported in 1835, but by then other textiles were already a prominent industry. The journalism/publishing element owes much

Dundee from the air, looking west. The numbers refer to the pages in this book on which that building or feature is illustrated.

to the success of DC Thomson, famed for comics such as 'The Beano', 'The Dandy' and its character 'Desperate Dan' (see p.4). Dundee also became an important centre for whaling and by 1859 the first custom-built whaler was in use by the Dundee fleet. Shipbuilding developed, with Scott of the Antarctic's vessel *Discovery* its most famous achievement. She returned to Dundee in 1986 and now forms the city's foremost tourist attraction.

The surrounding county of Angus has witnessed some of the most formative events in Scotland's history. The Battle of Dunnichen or Nechtansmere (near the village of Lethan) between the resident Picts and invading Northumbrians in 685 effectively stopped the Angles from moving north and thus helped to enable the subsequent creation of the Kingdom of Alba, later to become Scotland. According to historian Hector Boethe, King Malcolm III held the first Scottish Parliament in Forfar. In 1320, Arbroath Abbey was the scene of one of the most significant events in Scottish

6   RRS *Discovery*, launched in 1901, the first ship in the world to be designed specifically for scientific research.

history. On 6 April 1320, the Scottish Declaration of Independence was signed there by the assembled Scottish nobility, when the Scots declared their nationhood and right to self-government. These events are behind the 'Scotland's Birthplace' branding which appears around the county.

This book takes the reader on a roughly circular tour of the region beginning in Dundee. From there the coastal strip up to Montrose is explored, then turning inland we visit the towns that serve the fertile rural hinterland. No less than 40% of Scotland's Class 1 agricultural land is in Angus and 28% of Scotland's potatoes are grown here. Angus cattle are world-renowned for their delicious beef. To the north lie the beautiful Angus Glens which lead to the Braes of Angus, rising to over 914m/3000ft. These mountains form the south-eastern edge of the Cairngorms range and offer first-class hill walking and rock climbing. As will be seen, Dundee and Angus encapsulate all that is appealing in Scotland, from cultured city through rural tranquillity to wild-side adventure land!

The statue in Arbroath that commemorates the Declaration of Arbroath (see also p.40).

8 Central Dundee viewed from City Square. On the left, Reform Street runs down to the McManus Art
Gallery and Museum. High Street runs from left to right. The city centre of today still owes much to

the City Improvement Act of 1871, which swept away many run-down buildings from earlier times. 9

10 The Overgate Shopping Centre of today opened in 2000, replacing the 1960s original.
The name 'Overgate' comes from the street that used to run where the shops now stand.

Dundonians enjoy a summer day in the pleasant green space between the Steeple Church and 11 Nethergate. Through the trees is the Trades House Bar at the corner of Nethergate and Union Street.

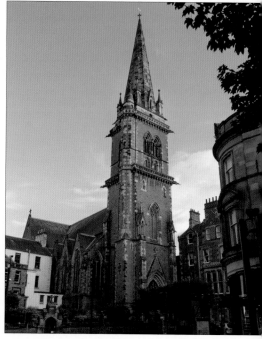

12 A contrast in church towers: left, the tower of the Steeple Church, Nethergate and right, the spire of St Paul's, High Street. Both these landmarks can be seen in the aerial picture on p.5.

The impressive interior of St Paul's Episcopal Cathedral. Designed by Sir George Gilbert Scott and completed in 1855, since 1905 it has been the Cathedral Church of the Diocese of Brechin.

14 Caird Hall in City Square is Dundee's principal concert hall. Although the foundation stone was laid in 1914, due to the First World War it did not open until 1923. It is named after Sir James Caird.

Left: Caird Hall at night. Right: this High Street building has amazingly survived since 1560. The
clock dates from 1932 and carries a model of the old Town House that once stood nearby (see p.19).

16 Dundee City Hall. In 1914, Sir James Caird, who had made a fortune through the jute trade in the city, pledged £100,000 for the building of a new City Hall and Council Chamber.

This project was not completed until 1933 and caused the demolition of various buildings including **17** the architecturally significant Town House of 1732. Pictured here is the Council Chamber.

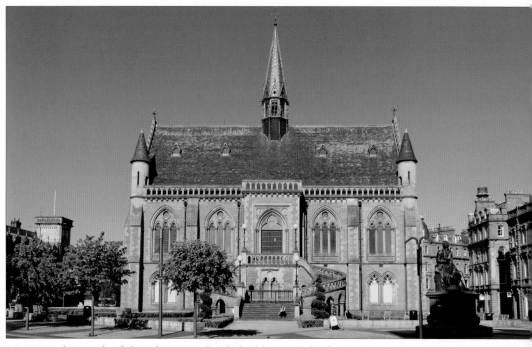

18 Housed in a splendid Gothic Revival-style building and displaying Dundee's main collection, The McManus Art Gallery and Museum has been at the heart of art and culture in the city since 1867.

Amongst its many fine exhibits is this model of the centre of Dundee c. 1850. The large building on the left is the 1732-built Town House that succumbed to the 1930s City Square redevelopment.

20 Unexpected creatures in the city centre: Dundee's Dragon, sculpted by Prentice Oliphant, lurks in Murraygate. Inset: mischievous monkey tampers with the Information Board.

This view looks across to the University of Dundee's campus at Airlie Place to the west of the **21** city centre. The small-scale bandstand is a replica of the full-size one at Magdalen Green.

22 Discovery Point is an all-weather, award-winning, 5-star attraction which features this tableau of the construction of *Discovery*, and of course the chance to explore the real thing!

Discovery is berthed in her own specially built dock. At the end of a showery day, the clouds help to **23** create a spectacular sunset above the city skyline.

24 Dundee Law provides grandstand views over the city and surrounding area. This is the scene to the east, looking across to Broughty Ferry, with Broughty Castle in its strategic coastal location

(see pages 36-37). In the Iron Age, Dundee Law was a hill fort. Today it is the suitably prominent location for the city's main War Memorial, erected in 1923 (see over).

26 Left: Dundee Law War Memorial. Right: 'Cox's Stack', the spectacular 86m/283ft chimney of the former Camperdown Jute Mill, built from coloured bricks in the style of an Italian campanile.

Also seen from Dundee Law, the spire of St Paul's Cathedral points heavenwards, while the traffic on **27** the adjacent Tay Road Bridge gives the impression that you can get there by car!

28 This view of the Tay Rail Bridge from Windsor Street (off Perth Road) telescopes its two mile/three km. length and gives an interesting impression of its construction.

Three scenes from HM Frigate *Unicorn*, one of the six oldest ships in the world, being launched in 1824. She is berthed in Dundee's Victoria Dock and is open to the public.

30 Verdant Works, West Henderson Wynd, is Scotland's Jute Museum. It weaves the tale of jute with the life and work of old Dundee, from the incredible rise of the industry to its subsequent decline.

During the 19th and early 20th centuries jute was indispensable. Its uses included sacking, ropes, boot linings, aprons, carpets, tents, roofing felt and much more. Pictured: the Machine Hall.

32 Dundee Botanic Garden is located in 9.5 hectares of south-facing land near the banks of the River Tay. These attractive walls are a feature that was added from 2006 to 2008.

The Garden is also home to this impressive sculpture by Ron Martin called 'The Bridge'. **33**
Inset: Peacock butterfly on blue agapanthus flowers.

34 Dundee is well endowed with many fine parks and gardens, one of which is Baxter Park on Arbroath Road, named after the Baxter family, flax mill owners, who gifted the park to the city in 1863.

Claypotts Castle, in the West Ferry area of Dundee, is an outstanding example of 16th-century Scottish architecture, which is both intact and little altered. Built 1569-1588 by John Strachan.

36 Broughty Ferry is a small port and residential suburb just east of Dundee. It used to be linked by ferry to Tayport in Fife and from 1854 operated the first 'roll on – roll off' train ferry.

Built in the late 15th century, Broughty Castle has been adapted through the years to meet the **37** nation's changing defence needs until 1932. Today it houses a museum run by Dundee City Council.

38 Moving a few miles east, this is Barry Mill, a traditional water-powered oatmeal mill. It operated commercially until 1982, the last of its kind in Angus, and is still run for demonstration purposes.

Returning to the coast, Carnoustie boasts four magnificent golf courses and regularly hosts top-level tournaments such as the Scottish Open. It provides a stern test for the world's best golfers.

40 A few miles up the coast from Carnoustie is Arbroath, one of Scotland's most historic towns. The abbey, founded in 1178 for monks of the Tironensian order by King William the Lion, with its

extensive red sandstone remains is a sight both impressive and inspiring. The picture shows the extent
of its southern elevation. The Declaration of Arbroath was signed here in 1320 (see introduction).

42 The abbot's house (seen towards the left on the previous page) is one of the most complete abbot's residences in Britain. Pictured here is its undercroft where stonework from the abbey is exhibited.

This view looks east along the remains of the nave, with visitors enjoying the tranquil atmosphere 43
and sense of history which pervade this lovely place.

44 Beside Arbroath's harbour stands this elegant complex of Regency buildings dating from 1813.
Now the Burgh's museum, until 1955 they formed the shore station for the Bell Rock Lighthouse.

Arbroath harbour. 'Arbroath Smokies', a locally originated smoked haddock delicacy, have become **45** prized throughout the world.

46 A few miles north of Arbroath lies Lunan Bay, perhaps the most perfect spot on the Angus coastline.
This is the north end of the bay, where the sea has eroded caves and rock arches into the cliffs.

This southwards view from above the bay presents the whole glorious two-mile vista that stretches 47 down to Eathie Haven. The Lunan Water flows into the sea behind the white building.

48 As mentioned in the introduction, potatoes are a major crop in Angus. Here, just inland from Lunan Bay on a fine May day, the ground is prepared for planting by some hi-tech equipment.

The town of Montrose is about three miles north of Lunan Bay. Left: statue of James Graham, **49** first Marquis of Montrose. Right: statue of Robert Burns at Middle Links, Montrose.

50 Early spring in Montrose, with crocuses adding colour to the graveyard of Montrose Old Church. The town stands on the spit of land between the Montrose basin and the sea.

Montrose Old Church was built in 1791 to replace an earlier, 16th-century structure and initially **51** seated 2,700 people. The impressive steeple seen here was added in 1834.

52 Hope Paton Park and Bowling Green, Montrose, were laid out c.1904 as an extension to the Mid Links thanks to the generosity of Miss Hope Henderson Paton and other members of her family.

This statue overlooking the beach is by Montrose sculptor and artist William Lamb, 1893-1951. **53**
His studio at 24 Market Street, Montrose, is now a museum to his life and work.

54 Montrose Basin is an enclosed estuary of the river South Esk covering 750 hectares, home to over 50,000 migratory birds. On the far side of the Basin, the House of Dun can just be seen . . .

. . . and here it is in close-up. This beautiful Georgian house, built in 1730 by William Adam, **55** features superb plasterwork. Outside, enjoy the attractive walled garden and woodland walks.

56 Now we turn west and head inland approximately 12 miles to White Caterthun hill fort, of which more later (see pages 63-64). From this elevated position, the character of the intervening landscape

can be appreciated. Amidst the variety of farming that is apparent in this early-September scene, the grain harvest has begun in some fields. In the distance are Montrose and its Basin.

58 Next stop is the pleasing town of Brechin. Pictured is Brechin Castle, reconstructed in the early 1700s and incorporating parts of the original castle dating back to the 13th century.

The Castle Garden is one of the finest private gardens in Scotland extending to over 40 acres of planted parkland and a walled garden. This is Azalea Walk, looking its best.

60 In Brechin Cathedral churchyard stands (left) this late-11th century Irish-style Round Tower, one of only two in Scotland. Centre: the Cathedral tower. Right: flowers in the Cathedral churchyard

The Caledonian Railway is a steam and diesel heritage railway on which visitors can ride for four miles between Brechin and Bridge of Dun. Here, a passenger train has just arrived at Brechin. 61

62 Textiles fuelled Brechin's 19thC growth, exemplified by Denburn Works, a linen mill built in 1864 and its finest industrial building. It ceased production in 1982 and has been turned into flats.

Now we take a closer look at the Caterthun hill forts. This is the earlier (Iron Age) Brown Caterthun, **63**
its name reflecting that it is an earthwork, comprising four concentric ramparts and ditches.

64 The principal work of the early Christian-era White Caterthun is a massive stone rampart, some of the remains of which can be seen in the foreground of this northwards view.

A short distance north-west from the Caterthuns, this is the picturesque planned village of Edzell. **65**
The grand Dalhousie Arch straddles the B966 from the south, framing the Inglis Memorial Hall.

66 Edzell Castle represents the more cultured side of lordly life in late medieval times. The seat of the Lindsay family, they built the castle in the 16th century. Inset: peacock at Edzell Castle.

The family's greatest building achievement at Edzell was the wonderful walled garden, the walls of 67 which display a series of unique carved panels and flower-filled niches.

68 Now it's time to start exploring the Angus Glens. Glen Esk, some 15 miles long, runs north from Edzell into the Cairngorm Mountains. We're heading for the more rugged terrain in the distance . . .

Glen Esk ends where the valley divides into Glens Mark and Lee. Heading up Glen Lee, we come to **69** the ruins of Loch Lee Old Church, with the waters of the loch choppy on this windy day.

70 Beyond Loch Lee the Water of Lee tumbles down from the hills to feed the loch, creating delightful scenes typical of Highland Scotland, especially so when the heather is in bloom.

Here the valleys divide again, with the Water of Unich coming in from the south-west and cascading down these impressive falls (left), with the view back from the top (right). **71**

72 A strenuous climb past the waterfalls and on up through the gorge of the Water of Unich ensues, followed by a boggy trudge up the slopes of Carn Lick. The effort is rewarded by this superb vista of

Glen Lee, from which the entire length of the walk back to Invermark can be enjoyed. From here, the route continues down the eastern slopes to Inchgrundle.

74 While descending Carn Lick, a minor diversion to the left of the path reveals the dramatic drop down to the corrie lochan.

Returning to more gentle country, this is Strathmore south-west of Brechin near Netherton. In this May picture, the promise of good crops is evident in the potato ridges and flowering oil-seed rape. **75**

76 Angus has many Pictish sculptured stones, some of the finest of which are in the village of Aberlemno between Brechin and Forfar. Two of them are pictured here.

Restenneth Priory, a house of Augustinian canons, is situated a couple of miles east of Forfar in this peaceful setting. The lower part of the tower is very early Romanesque work.

78 The Town and County Hall pictured here reflects that Forfar is the administrative centre of Angus, following on from its role as county town of Forfarshire, as Angus was known from the

18th century until 1928. Forfar is an ancient settlement, with origins that probably go back to **79** Pictish times. Today it is a town which sustains some pleasingly traditional shops, as seen above.

80 About five miles south-west of Forfar stands Glamis Castle, undoubtedly one of Scotland's finest as this spectacular aerial view demonstrates. The book's front cover picture is the 'classic' view.

As the ancestral home of the Earls of Strathmore, Glamis Castle has witnessed more than 600 years
of the nation's history. Above: the crypt is full of historic artefacts.

82 There are many aspects to the Castle's extensive grounds. This is the Italian Garden, created by the late Queen Mother's parents in 1910.

Left: detail of a fountain in the Italian Garden. Right: the Princess Margaret Memorial in the gardens of Glamis Castle.

84 The village of Glamis grew up around the castle, providing all the necessary services for its royal inhabitants. Here, at the village centre, is the Mercat Cross and corner shop.

Just round the corner from the shop is the Angus Folk Museum. The domestic section is housed in **85** this row of six charming 18th-century cottages. The agricultural collection is opposite.

86 We now move about five miles north to the town of Kirriemuir. The town centre square seen here is bounded to the right by the former Town House, now the Gateway to the Glens Museum.

Left: a statue of Peter Pan also graces the square as his creator, J.M. Barrie, was born in Kirriemuir. **87**
Right: Kirriemuir's Millennium Sculpture 'The Circle of Time' by Bruce Walker.

88 J.M. Barrie's Birthplace recreates some of the cottage's rooms as they would have been in 1860 when he was born. Visitors can also enjoy rooms that reflect Peter Pan's adventures.

In 1930 J.M. Barrie donated a Camera Obscura, and the cricket pavilion in which it sits, **89** to the town. From its location on Kirrie Hill there are fine views of the surrounding countryside.

90 East of Kirriemuir in Glen Isla is the Reekie Linn waterfall. One of the most spectacular and accessible in Scotland, the total drop seen here is one of 24m/79ft in a gorge up to 45m/150ft deep.

For the last leg of this journey we turn north to the Angus Glens once more. Glen Prosen, **91** one of the smaller glens, lies between Glen Isla and Glen Clova and is a joy to explore.

92 Travelling up the 18-mile length of Glen Clova is a journey into an increasingly dramatic landscape. Here, near the head of the glen, autumn tints and early snow add their colours to the scene.

A winter walk from Clova village up into the hills reveals a partly frozen Loch Brandy. The shadow shows that the sun is already low; the back cover picture was taken from here soon after.

94 This view looks into spectacular Glen Doll, which is in effect an extension of Glen Clova. The route to the Munros (Scottish hills above 914m/3000ft) Driesh and Mayar heads this way.

The view from the end of the road in Glen Doll. But it's no terminus for those prepared to continue on foot. You can walk through to Aberdeenshire from here, but that's another journey . . .

Published 2013 by Ness Publishing, 47 Academy Street, Elgin, Moray, IV30 1LR
Phone 01343 549663   www.nesspublishing.co.uk

All photographs © Colin Nutt except p.5 © Guthrie Aerial Photography; p.31 © Dundee Heritage Trust, Verdant Works; pp.80 & 81 © Glamis Castle. Thanks to Dundee Art Galleries and Museums (Dundee City Council) for their co-operation with the picture on p.19.

Text © Colin Nutt
ISBN 978-1-906549-23-7

Front cover: Glamis Castle; p.1: snow sculpture, Braes of Angus; p.4: statue of 'Desperate Dan'; this page: 'Mechanical Horse' at Brechin station; back cover: winter evening, Glen Clova

For a list of websites and phone numbers please turn over > > > >

Websites and phone numbers (where available) for principal places featured in this book in alphabetical order:

Aberlemno Sculptured Stones: www.historic-scotland.gov.uk
Angus Folk Museum: www.nts.org.uk/property/angus-folk-museum (T) 0844 493 2141
Angus Glens: www.angusglens.co.uk
Angus: www.angusahead.com
Arbroath Abbey: www.historic-scotland.gov.uk (T) 01241 878756
Arbroath Smokies: www.arbroathsmokies.net
Barry Mill: www.nts.org.uk (T) 0844 493 2140
Brechin Castle: www.dalhousieestates.co.uk (T) 01356 624566
Brechin Cathedral Round Tower: www.historic-scotland.gov.uk
Brechin Cathedral: www.brechincathedral.org (T) 01356 629360
Broughty Castle: www.leisureandculturedundee.com (T) 01382 436916
Broughty Ferry: www.cometobroughty.co.uk
Caird Hall: www.cairdhall.co.uk (T) 01382 434451
Caledonian Railway: caledonianrailway.com (T) 01356 622992
Carnoustie Golf Links: www.carnoustiegolflinks.co.uk (T) 01241 802270
Caterthun hill forts: www.historic-scotland.gov.uk
City Hall: www.dundeecity.gov.uk (T) 01382 434000
Claypotts Castle: www.historic-scotland.gov.uk (T) 01786 431324
Den Burn Works: www.brechin-angus.co.uk/brechin/places
Discovery Point: www.rrsdiscovery.com (T) 01382 309060
Dundee University Botanic Garden: www.dundee.ac.uk/botanic (T) 01382 381190
Dundee: www.dundee.com (T) 01382 434252
Edzell Castle: www.historic-scotland.gov.uk (T) 01356 648631